NINJA KID 10

NINJA HEROES!

Scholastic Press
An imprint of Scholastic Australia Pty Limited (ABN 11 000 614 577)
PO Box 579 Gosford NSW 2250
www.scholastic.com.au

Part of the Scholastic Group
Sydney • Auckland • New York • Toronto • London • Mexico City • New Delhi • Hong Kong • Buenos Aires • Puerto Rico

First published by Scholastic Australia in 2022.

A catalogue record for this book is available from the National Library of Australia

Typeset in Bizzle-Chizzle, featuring Hola Bisou and Handblock.

ISBN 978-93-5471-899-1

This reprint edition: November 2025

Printed in India at MicroPrints India, New Delhi

ANH DO

illustrated by Anton Emdin

NINJA KID 10

NINJA HEROES!

A Scholastic Press book
from Scholastic Australia

ONE

Hi! I'm **Nelson Kane**. Until I turned ten, I was just your typical kid. Actually, I was your typical NERD!

Then, on my tenth birthday, something completely NUTS happened. I woke up with **CRAZY NINJA SKILLS!**

Now, whenever our town's in trouble, I turn into

NiNJA KiD!

The rest of the time I'm still a bit of a NERD.

My **ninja powers** come from my **dad**, who went missing when I was a baby.

For the longest time, **no-one** had any clue where my dad was. But I think I know what's happened to him. And who's responsible . . .

My dad's evil twin brother,

ANDREW KANE.

When the twins turned ten, Andrew was **angry** he didn't get ninja powers like my dad. To make up for it, my grandma taught him how to `invent` things.

I think Grandma is the **BEST** inventor in the world. Even though her inventions don't always work out as planned.

Like the bike helmet with built-in air conditioning. Only problem is, it's so powerful it **FREEZES** your hair!

Or the 'Never Lose It' super ball, which always comes back even if it bounces too far away. The only problem is, you never know **when** it's going to come back!

Or the car-washing **ROBOT,** which is **awesome** at making your car spotless and clean.

Only problem is, it sometimes cleans the driver, too!

Grandma taught Andrew **everything** she knew about inventing. But instead of being grateful, Andrew **stole** her inventions and became the **evil genius** known as **DOCTOR KANE!**

Dr Kane wants everyone to leave **Duck Creek** so he can mine our little town for **rare purple stones.** These stones give him the power to control other people's thoughts.

So far, Dr Kane has unleashed **evil toys, mechanical flying beasts** and even a **giant squid** on Duck Creek to try and get rid of us all.

Dr Kane doesn't act alone. He has an evil chipmunk sidekick, named **EINSTEIN.** And another helper, known as the

ULTIMATE NINJA.

I think the Ultimate Ninja is actually **my DAD!** My theory is that Dr Kane kidnapped his twin brother and brainwashed him, using the powers of the purple stones.

One day, I'm going to rescue my dad and bring him **home.**

Home is a **junkyard** in **Duck Creek** that I share with my mum, Grandma, my cousin Kenny and our dog, **Noodles** the Moodle!

When I become Ninja Kid, Kenny becomes **H-DUDE**. Apparently, the 'H' stands for **handsome!**

As Ninja Kid and H-Dude, Kenny and I use our powers to protect Duck Creek from evil.

We don't act alone either. Our friends, **Sarah** and **Tiffany,** are always there to help keep the baddies away!

Sarah and Tiffany have **no idea** that **Ninja Kid** and **H-Dude** are actually me and Kenny.

They just think we have terrible timing and always miss the action!

TWO

Even when Kenny and I aren't Ninja Kid and H-Dude, we do everything together. Right now, we're desperate to get a role in our class play, which is based on our favourite ever book series . . .

The *Pow Pow Pig* books are about an awesome pig named Pow Pow, and his fantastic friends, Cha Cha Chicken, Kung Fu Duck and Barry the Goat.

They are from the future, 2050 to be exact, and they travel through time, solving mysteries, righting wrongs and making the world a **better place!**

Kenny and I have read the *Pow Pow* books **heaps** of times so we didn't think we needed to prepare for the auditions. But as we watched everyone else, we began to seriously regret our decision.

Sarah and Tiffany had been getting ready for their auditions for weeks. And it showed.

Tiffany was auditioning for the role of Cha Cha Chicken. She nailed Cha Cha's **swagger** and she had even made her own version of Cha Cha's Mixy-Fixy tool – an **incredible gizmo** that is every tool in one!

Sarah was trying out for the part of Kung Fu Duck. She had Kung Fu's quick wit down pat.

And she'd totally mastered Kung Fu's special move – flicking a tea towel like a **whip!**

Billy Bob was hoping to play Pow Pow Pig. Not only did he dress up as Pow Pow, but he also brought along Wally, his llama, dressed as Barry the Goat!

Kenny and I thought Billy Bob's audition was **amazing.** But Mr Fletcher didn't seem too impressed. Especially when Billy Bob's llama **pooped** on the gym floor!

You'll need to clean that up, Billy Bob.

'No **prob-llama!**' Billy Bob answered with a cheeky grin.

Charles was auditioning to play both Pow Pow and Barry the Goat.

'I'm such a good actor,' Charles said, 'I can easily play both characters.'

Charles had arrived with his family's butler, who wheeled a full set into the gym!

I was **desperate** to play the role of Pow Pow Pig. And Kenny was **super keen** to play Barry the Goat. But Billy Bob and Charles were so good. How could we compete?

It was finally time to audition. After watching everyone else, we were **super nervous.**

'I really wish we prepared for this!' I said.

'Me too,' Kenny said. 'I'm more nervous than a mouse at a cat's birthday party!'

Our knees were **knocking** as we made our way towards the stage . . .

then the bell rang!

'Lunchtime is over, back to class,' Mr Fletcher said. 'We'll do the rest of the auditions tomorrow.'

Kenny and I couldn't have been more relieved!

THREE

When Kenny and I arrived home from school, we heard **shrieks** of joy coming from Grandma's workshop.

'Sounds like Grandma is cooking up a new invention,' I said.

'Let's check it out,' Kenny replied, pulling a bunch of bananas from his backpack and shoving one in his mouth.

Did I mention that Kenny is **always** hungry?

Sometimes he has such a **BIG** breakfast, he doesn't finish it until lunchtime!

Grandma was so focused on her new invention, she didn't notice us stepping into her workshop.

'Hi, Grandma!' Kenny said.

Grandma was so shocked, she almost jumped through the roof!

'Sorry, boys, I was in **the zone,'** Grandma said when she finally looked up. 'How did your auditions go?'

'We don't have our turn until tomorrow,' Kenny said.

'Which is a **good** thing,' I added, 'because we weren't ready.'

'You can never be too prepared,' Grandma replied, wisely.

'What are you working on, Grandma?' I asked.

'Looks like a *super-fancy* camera,' Kenny said.

'It's a lot fancier than a camera,' Grandma replied. 'I call it the **CHARACTER CAMERA.**'

'Awesome! What does it do, Grandma?' I asked.

'My invention brings **book characters to life.**'

'You've invented some **incredible** things, Grandma,' I said. 'But making book characters come to life? That has to be impossible!'

'Totally impossible,' Kenny added.

'Prepare to be amazed, boys,' Grandma said.

She picked up a book called **Monkey Business** and aimed the Character Camera at it.

Kenny and I couldn't believe it. The chimpanzee leapt out of the book and began **jumping** around the workshop!

'This is **unbelievable**, Grandma!' I exclaimed.

'Amazing!' Kenny agreed. 'I can't believe what I'm **chimpan-seeing!**'

The chimpanzee leapt onto Kenny's head, **snatched** the bunch of bananas out of his hand, and shoved one in its mouth!

'He loves eating, just like me!' Kenny said, smiling.

'I think we've found your **long-lost chimp brother,** Kenny!' I laughed.

Next, the chimpanzee grabbed onto the light and swung backwards and forwards. Then it started **throwing bananas** around the workshop.

'Maybe a **cheeky chimp** wasn't the best character to bring to life!' Grandma said, chasing it around the workshop.

The chimpanzee was just about to **leap out** the workshop door when Grandma picked up the Character Camera, switched it to **reverse** and aimed it at the chimp.

Just like that, the chimpanzee returned to the book! It was **Strange** seeing the cheeky chimp back on the page, inside its story once again.

'This is definitely your **coolest** invention ever, Grandma,' I said.

'**ICE COLD!**' Kenny agreed.

'I just need to work on the battery,' Grandma said. 'At this stage, it can only charge for a few minutes.'

'You'll work it out, Grandma,' I said.

'You always do,' Kenny added.

That night, Kenny and I took Grandma's advice about preparing and we learnt our audition scenes off by heart. Then we practised Pow Pow Pig and Barry the Goat's signature moves.

'Grandma would be **proud** of us,' I said. 'We've done everything we can to prepare for our auditions.'

'Not **EVERYTHING**,' Kenny replied with a glint in his eye.

'If we really want to get in character,' Kenny said, 'we should **talk** to Pow Pow and the gang.'

'Speak to the books?' I asked, confused.

'No,' Kenny said. 'Bring them **to life** with the Character Camera!'

'Great idea,' I said. 'Let's ask Grandma.'

Kenny and I ran into the lounge room. Even though the TV was blaring, Mum and Grandma were both **snoring** on the couch!

'Should we wake her up?' Kenny asked, looking at Grandma.

'No way,' I replied. 'She's had a huge day of inventing. She needs rest.'

'She wouldn't mind if we **borrowed** the Character Camera for a little bit,' Kenny said.

'Mucking around with Grandma's inventions **always** gets us in **trouble**,' I replied.

'We're not **mucking** around,' Kenny said. 'We're using the Character Camera to **prepare** for our auditions. Remember what Grandma said . . . you can never be too prepared.'

Kenny was **awesome** at talking people into stuff. He's going to make a great salesman one day!

'Alright,' I said. 'Let's go get the Character Camera.'

'Great idea, Nelson!' Kenny said.

'Hey, it was your idea!' I replied.

'It doesn't matter whose idea it was,' Kenny said. **'Let's do it!'**

We grabbed the Character Camera from Grandma's workshop and brought it back to our room. Kenny opened our favourite *Pow Pow Pig* book.

I aimed the Character Camera at the page.

Even though we'd seen Grandma's invention work with the chimp, Kenny and I couldn't believe our eyes when Pow Pow Pig, Barry the Goat, Cha Cha Chicken and Kung Fu Duck leapt out of the book and **INTO OUR ROOM!**

'I can't believe you're all actually here,' I said.

'This is **beyond awesome,'** Kenny said.

'It's **awesome times awesome!'** Pow Pow said.

'Thanks for bringing us here,' Cha Cha Chicken said.

'We love **exploring** new worlds,' Kung Fu Duck said.

'As long as there's tasty food on offer!' Barry the Goat added.

'I love food, too!' Kenny laughed.

'Have you got a **mystery** for us to solve?' Pow Pow asked.

'Or a wrong to be righted?' Cha Cha added.

'Ah, not exactly,' I said. 'We're auditioning to play Pow Pow and Barry in our class play and we want to learn how to be **just like you!**'

'What about me and Cha Cha?' Kung Fu Duck asked.

'Yeah!' Cha Cha said. 'We're the **best** characters!'

'Our friends Sarah and Tiffany are hoping to play you,' I said.

'They did brilliant auditions,' Kenny said. 'If they get the parts, they'll do you proud.'

'No substitute for the original,' Cha Cha said with a wink.

'So you want some tips on playing me?' Pow Pow asked.

'Love some!' I replied.

'It's not easy,' Pow Pow said. 'You need to find a subtle mix of **charm**, **humour** and **BROOMSTICK SPINNING!** Just start by working on this one move, and you'll be on your way.'

'My character is a lot more complex,' Barry told Kenny. 'You need to be **funny, FEARLESS, HUNGRY** and know how to wrangle a rake!'

'I'm definitely funny, fearless and hungry,' said Kenny. 'If I **practise, practise, practise** with the rake, I'll be all set!'

'That's all super helpful,' I said.

'Totally!' Kenny added. 'Want to stick around and **watch our play?** It's on tomorrow night.'

'That sounds like a ton of fun,' Pow Pow replied. 'But we need to get back in the book.'

'We're in the middle of battling the evil ***MUZZKITO,***' Kung Fu said.

'He seems nasty,' I said.

'Could you **zap us back** into the book?' Pow Pow asked.

'Sure can,' I said. 'Thanks for all your help.'

'Sorry to see you go,' Kenny said. 'I **miss you** all already!'

'We're right here **any time** you need us,' Kung Fu said, gesturing to the book.

I aimed the Character Camera at Pow Pow and the gang. **FLASH!**

Just like that, they were all back in the book.

Kenny and I practised our lines several more times. We found it so much easier to get into character after meeting Pow Pow and Barry the Goat. Now we couldn't wait for our audition.

‘One more sleep!’ Kenny said, excitedly. ‘I’ve got a **really good feeling** about this!’

FOUR

Kenny and I had planned to tell Grandma and Mum at breakfast that we'd used the Character Camera. But we **slept in!** We barely had time to throw down breakfast before it was time to rush out the door.

'We'll tell Mum and Grandma as soon as we get home,' I said, as we arrived at the school gates.

'Hopefully we can soften them up by telling them we **got the parts** of Pow Pow and Barry in the school play,' Kenny replied.

The audition went **even better** than Kenny and I could have imagined. Not only did we remember all our lines, we **nailed** our performances! But it was still a nervous wait before Mr Fletcher announced who had got the roles.

'The standard of auditions was **exceptional,'** Mr Fletcher said. 'Seems you all really love Pow Pow Pig and his friends.'

Our whole class cheered.

'Let's get straight into it,' Mr Fletcher continued. 'Playing the part of Cha Cha Chicken in tomorrow night's school play will be . . .

Tiffany.'

Tiffany jumped up excitedly and **twirled** her Mixy-Fixy above her head.

'Playing the part of Kung Fu Duck,' Mr Fletcher said, 'will be . . . **Sarah!**'

'Woohoo!' Sarah flicked her tea towel excitedly.

'Now, to the role of Pow Pow Pig . . .' Mr Fletcher continued.

I was so nervous, I was shaking like a Chihuahua in an **ICE BATH!**

'Pow Pow will be played by . . . **Charles Brock!'** Mr Fletcher said.

'Yes!' Charles said, jumping to his feet and thumping his chest.

My heart **SANK** to the floor.

'Wait!' Mr Fletcher said. 'I looked at the wrong piece of paper. Playing the part of Pow Pow Pig will be . . . **Nelson Kane.'**

I couldn't believe it. Neither could Charles.

'I want a re-count!' he yelled.

'There's nothing to re-count,' Mr Fletcher said. 'I just got my notes muddled.'

'Next up, the role of Barry the Goat.' Mr Fletcher paused for effect. 'And that role goes to . . . **Charles Brock!**'

'Oh no, I've done it again,' Mr Fletcher said. 'I really need to sort these notes out. Playing Barry the Goat will be . . . **Kenny!**'

Charles looked like he was about to explode.

But Kenny was overjoyed. '**Baaaa!**' he bleated excitedly.

Mr Fletcher announced the other parts. Billy Bob got the role of Muzzkito, which he was pumped about.

Charles was given the part of 'Tree Number Three'. He was **NOT** happy about it.

We only had time for **one** big rehearsal before the play, but it was a ton of fun.

After the rehearsal, Mr Fletcher told us to look after our costumes overnight. So we all walked home in them to stop them from getting scrunched up in our school bags!

It must have been a strange sight because everyone **beeped** their horns and **cheered** as they drove past.

Then we heard a strange **buzzing** noise.

It was growing **LOUDER** by the second.

'Sounds like a mosquito,' Sarah said.

'Not just one mosquito,' Tiffany said.

'I hate mosquitoes,' Sarah said.

'Seems they hate us, too!' Tiffany said, pointing over our heads.

The mosquitoes were heading straight for us.

RUN!!!

The mosquitoes weren't just chasing us, they were **trying to bite us!**

We ran in and out of the bushes to avoid the angry swarm. Kenny and I would have loved to turn into Ninja Kid and H-Dude, but we couldn't reveal our secret identities to Sarah and Tiffany.

By the time we got home, we were itchy all over from mosquito bites!

Not only were we itchy, we were also worried.

'It's not mosquito season,' Kenny said. 'Where did they come from?'

'And why were they **targeting** us?' I asked.

That evening, the mosquito swarm was the main story on the local news. The swarm had grown even bigger now – it looked like a **GIANT angry cloud** buzzing above Duck Creek.

Things got even more **bizarre** when a tiny figure snatched the microphone off the news reporter.

'Whoa,' I uttered, staring at the tiny critter on the screen. **'That's Muzzkito!'**

'That is **NOT** good news,' Kenny added.

'Who's Muzzkito?' Grandma asked.

'He's from those books you love, isn't he?' Mum asked.

Kenny and I suddenly had a **TERRIBLE** realisation.

'We must have accidentally brought Muzzkito to life when we zapped the *Pow Pow* book,' I whispered to Kenny.

'This is bad,' Kenny replied. '**This is REALLY bad.**'

'Something **strange** is in the air,' Muzzkito said to the reporter.

'You're talking about your **mosquitoes?'** the reporter asked.

'They're not strange, they're beautiful!' Muzzkito said. 'What's strange is that I was in the middle of battling Pow Pow Pig and his friends when **ZAP!** I suddenly found myself in your boring town.'

'Rude little thing, isn't he?' Grandma said.

'This afternoon,' Muzzkito continued, 'I saw Pow Pow and his friends casually walking down the street as if everything was happy days. **Well, it's not!** Pow Pow, you and your annoying friends better meet me at Duck Creek Park at midday tomorrow or all hell will break loose!'

'What exactly do you mean by that threat?' the reporter asked.

'We need to tell Mum and Grandma what we've done,' I whispered to Kenny.

'They'll be **seriously cranky,**' Kenny replied.

'They'll be a lot crankier if Duck Creek is **overrun by mosquitoes,**' I said.

'What are you two whispering about?' Mum asked.

'You both look very **guilty,**' Grandma added.

Kenny and I shared a small nod then told Mum and Grandma EVERYTHING.

Mum and Grandma were disappointed, but not as CRANKY as Kenny and I expected.

'I wish you didn't use the Character Camera without asking me,' Grandma said. 'But what's done is done.'

'Should we use it again to bring Pow Pow and the gang back to battle Muzzkito?' I asked.

'It's still charging,' Grandma replied. 'It won't be ready for at least **24 hours**.'

'You'll have to go and meet Muzzkito,' Mum said, 'and tell him what you've done.'

'Then once the battery is charged, we'll zap him back into the book,' Grandma said.

That night, Kenny and I had trouble falling asleep. I was **super stressed** about the horrible mess we'd got Duck Creek into.

Kenny was worried about the school play.

'What if it's cancelled because of Muzzkito?' Kenny said. 'Barry the Goat is the role I was **born to play!**'

'Muzzkito's an **ANGRY** little dude,' I said. 'He won't listen to a couple of kids.'

'He has to,' Kenny replied. 'The thought of Duck Creek being overrun . . . that would be terrible. **Almost as terrible as running out of food!**'

FIVE

The next morning, Kenny and I ate an extra **BIG** breakfast to prepare for our encounter with Muzzkito. Kenny downed a huge glass of lemon juice then stuffed half a dozen cinnamon donuts into his mouth.

'Interesting breakfast choice!' I said.

'Mosquitoes are **repelled** by lemon and cinnamon,' Kenny said. 'If things get ugly with Muzzkito, my breath will be a **secret weapon!'**

Classic Kenny. He could always find a way to justify eating **loads of donuts!**

As soon as we'd finished breakfast, Kenny and I turned into **NINJA KID** and **H-DUDE.**

In the *Pow Pow* book, the gang stopped Muzzkito's army from biting them by wearing extra clothing. So Kenny and I made sure we had **more layers** than the world's biggest onion!

Mum and Grandma helped us get ready for our meeting with Muzzkito. Mum stuffed our backpacks full of mosquito spray and mosquito coils. Then she made sure we were covered in mosquito repellent.

Grandma handed us something that looked like a **normal pen.** But when you clicked the bottom of the pen, a giant **mosquito swatter** popped out of it.

Kenny and I made our way to Duck Creek Park and arrived a few minutes before twelve o'clock. The park was usually packed on a Saturday morning, but today it was **completely empty.**

Everyone had been scared away by Muzzkito.

But there was no sign of the **man-insect.**

The Duck Creek clock **chimed** twelve. That's when we heard the **buzzing**.

Softly at first. Then so **LOUD** Kenny and I could barely hear ourselves think. The cloud of mosquitoes had grown even larger!

It was so big it almost blackened the sky. And at the front of the horde was Muzzkito.

Muzzkito looked down at us and scrunched his tiny face. He seemed to be yelling, but his voice was so small we couldn't hear it.

'Are you talking to us?' I asked.

Muzzkito continued yelling, but we couldn't hear him above the buzz of the mosquitoes.

Muzzkito speared towards us then stopped and flapped his tiny wings right in front of our faces.

'**Can you hear me now?!**' he screamed angrily.

'Just!' Kenny said.

Muzzkito screwed up his face again before screaming, 'You're not Pow Pow Pig!' Then he turned to Kenny. 'And you're not Barry the Goat!'

'Very observant of you,' Kenny replied.

'They're all in the book you escaped from,' I said. 'What you saw yesterday were some kids **dressed up** as Pow Pow and his friends for a school play.'

'Don't worry,' I said to Muzzkito. 'We can get you **back into the book.** And you can continue your battle with Pow Pow and his friends.'

'I'm **never** going back in the book,' Muzzkito replied. 'I'm having too much fun bringing **terror** to your town!' He cackled again.

'I liked it better when we couldn't hear him,' Kenny whispered.

'What have you got against Duck Creek?' I asked.

'Nothing,' Muzzkito replied. 'I just love **destroying** places with my mosquitoes. It gives me a real **buzz!**'

He looked up to the swarm in the sky then shouted, 'Mosquitoes . . .

The mosquitoes moved as one towards us. Kenny and I clicked our pens and our **GIANT mosquito swatters** sprung out. Then we leapt high into the air and swatted as hard as we could.

We knocked dozens of mozzies to the ground! But there were so many more. And we'd made them **ANGRY!**

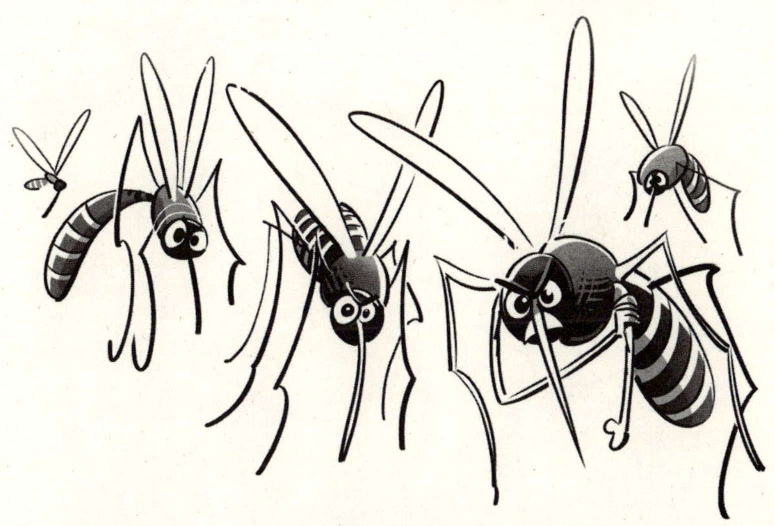

'You think a couple of oversized swatters can stop my **mozzie army**?' Muzzkito yelled.

'That was the plan,' Kenny said.

'But we have a few **other tricks** up our sleeve,' I added.

I plucked my ninja stars out of my backpack and drenched them in mosquito spray. Then I hurled them at the swarm.

Kenny brought down mosquitoes with a more unusual weapon . . .

his lemon-and-cinnamon-flavoured breath!

I sprayed repellent on my foot, then **JUMPED** high in the air and did a spinning kick which wiped out a big bunch of mosquitoes. Kenny waved a **red** handkerchief at the rest.

'What are you doing?' I asked. **'Theyre not bulls!'**

'True,' he said. 'But mosquitoes are also **attracted** to red!'

Kenny was right; the mosquitoes flew straight towards the red handkerchief. Then he hit them with mosquito spray!

'Olé!' said Kenny, clicking his fingers above his head triumphantly.

'Imbeciles!' Muzzkito screamed at what remained of his mosquito swarm.

Muzzkito's angry words stirred something in his mozzie army. They formed the shape of a **PITCHFORK** and speared towards us.

'I'm normally **happy** to see a fork,' said Kenny, 'but not when these mozzies are planning to make a **meal out of US!**'

Kenny and I tried all our tricks to fend them off.

NINJA KICKS! **GIANT SWATTERS!**

NINJA STARS!

MOSQUITO REPELLENT!

AND KENNY'S BREATH!

But **NOTHING** could stop the mosquitoes. They charged towards us and even though we were covered in layers of clothing and mosquito repellent, they bit us **EVERYWHERE!**

SiX

As Kenny and I writhed on the ground in pain, we heard a familiar sound above.

WHOOP!
WHOOP! WHOOP!

We looked up to see Dr Kane's helicopter approaching.

The only **good thing** about seeing Dr Kane is that he's usually with the **ULTIMATE NINJA,** who I'm pretty sure is my dad. But today, Dr Kane was alone. He didn't even have his evil chipmunk sidekick with him.

'Well, well, well,' Dr Kane yelled from the helicopter. 'If it isn't **Whingey Kid** and **Lame-Dude.**'

'Hey, Doctor **Pain-in-the-butt**,' Kenny replied.

Kenny and I were expecting Dr Kane to kick us while we were down. Instead, he turned his attention to Muzzkito.

'Hey, little man! Want to make a deal?'

Muzzkito flew higher, right in front of Dr Kane's nose. 'That depends. Who are you? And what do **you want** from me?'

'My name is Dr Kane and I have an offer you can't refuse.'

'If you **help me** scare everyone out of Duck Creek,' Dr Kane continued, 'I'll give you anything you want!'

'**Anything?**' Muzzkito replied.

'Within reason,' Dr Kane said. 'I'm a very powerful man, but even I have my limits. What did you have in mind, Muzzkito?'

'I dream of a world where people *love* mosquitoes as much as they love butterflies, and the trees are made of **ice-cream**,' Muzzkito replied.

'I was hoping for something a little more realistic,' Dr Kane grumbled.

'Fine,' Muzzkito replied. 'I've always hated being tiny. I want to be **HUGE.** But I'm guessing you can't make that happen either.'

'I've turned spiders into giant arachnids,' Dr Kane boasted. 'Of course I can make you bigger!'

'Whoa, whoa, whoa!' Muzzkito yelled. 'What are you pointing at me?'

'You've never seen a Zap-O-Matic?' Dr Kane replied.

Kenny and I had seen one before. Because Dr Kane stole the invention from Grandma!

He fired the Zap-O-Matic at Muzzkito.

Muzzkito was now a SIX-FOOT-TALL

FLYING MOSQUITO!

Muzzkito couldn't believe his eyes. Or his body!

'Look at me!' he boasted. 'I'm a **GIANT!** I'm king of the world!'

Muzzkito briefly stopped looking at his new muscles to ask Dr Kane, 'Can you make my mozzie friends bigger, too?'

'You're pushing your luck,' Dr Kane said.

'I can't get rid of all the humans in Duck Creek by myself,' Muzzkito replied.

'Fine,' Dr Kane agreed. He pointed his Zap-O-Matic at the cloud of mosquitoes above.

Kenny and I stared in **horror** at the sky, which was now full of **GIANT mosquitoes.**

'Look at the size of those things!' said Kenny. 'I should have eaten **a LOT** more donuts!'

'My part of the deal's done,' Dr Kane said. 'I'll be back once you've rid this town of pesky humans.' His helicopter banked, then disappeared into the distance.

But Kenny and I weren't worried about Dr Kane. We had **BIGGER,** buzzier problems.

We were a good match for a swarm of normal-sized mosquitoes. But a horde of human-sized mosquitoes was too tall an order. **Literally!**

The flapping of their oversized wings was almost deafening.

'Alright, my **giant bitey friends,'** Muzzkito yelled at his large mosquito army. 'Let's see what you can do now. **ATTACK!'**

'I was really hoping he wouldn't say that!' Kenny whispered.

'Me too,' I replied as the giant mosquitoes swarmed towards us. **'Drop and roll!'**

Kenny and I dropped to the dirt and **ninja rolled** away from the spearing mosquitoes, narrowly avoiding their giant angry stingers.

As we returned to our feet, we heard movement all around us. Human movement.

The people of Duck Creek had seen the huge mozzie swarm and had come to see what was happening. Sarah and Tiffany were among them.

'Ninja Kid! H-Dude!' Sarah said as they rushed over to us. 'How did the mosquitoes get so big?'

'You can thank Dr Kane for that **creepy** update,' Kenny replied.

'What can we do to help?' Tiffany asked.

'What we really need,' I said, 'is Pow Pow Pig and the gang. They'd know how to defeat Muzzkito.'

'Hate to tell you this,' Sarah said, 'but Pow Pow Pig and his friends are characters from a book. **They're not real!**'

'Psssst!' someone whispered from a nearby bush. Kenny and I recognised the voice. **It was Grandma!**

'We can't let Tiffany and Sarah see us with Grandma,' I whispered to Kenny. 'It could give away our identity.'

'Good call!' Kenny said. 'I'll **distract** them while you see what Grandma is up to.'

As Kenny chatted to Sarah and Tiffany, I quietly joined Grandma in the shrubbery.

'What are you doing here, Grandma?' I whispered.

'The Character Camera is fully charged and I've brought a *Pow Pow* book so you can **zap** Muzzkito back into it.'

'You're a **lifesaver,** Grandma!' I said.

I aimed the Character Camera at Muzzkito . . . **FLASH!**

But he easily dodged it.

I tried again. **FLASH!**

Muzzkito laughed as he easily flew out of the way. 'That's the **best you've got, kid?!'**

'Might have to go with **Plan B,** Grandma,' I said.

'Sure thing,' Grandma said. 'What's Plan B?'

'Bringing Pow Pow and the gang back to help.'

'Excellent idea,' Grandma replied.

She looked around at the **giant mosquitoes** who were chasing the people of Duck Creek out of town. 'Looks like you need my size converter, too.'

'To make me and Kenny **BIGGER?'** I asked.

'No. We can put it in **shrink** mode and zap those mosquitoes back to normal size. I'll head back to my workshop and grab it.'

Before I could respond, Grandma **zoomed off** on her banana-powered bike.

SEVEN

As Grandma rode away, I opened the book to a page featuring Pow Pow, Cha Cha, Barry and Kung Fu in battle mode. I aimed the Character Camera and . . .

It worked! My **HEROES** were standing in front of me again!

'We're back in Duck Creek,' Pow Pow said, a little surprised.

'Hey, you look familiar,' Barry said, studying me.

'I get that a lot,' I said nervously.

I couldn't risk them knowing that **Ninja Kid** and **Nelson** were the same person!

'What can we do for you?' Cha Cha asked.

'Help us stop Muzzkito and his mozzie army from **scaring away** our whole town,' I said.

As I led Pow Pow and the gang over to the others, Sarah and Tiffany couldn't believe their eyes.

'How is this **possible?**' Sarah asked, gobsmacked.

'You're my hero!' Tiffany said to Cha Cha.

'I get that a lot!' Cha Cha replied cheekily.

'Look who's finally arrived,' Muzzkito called down to Pow Pow. 'Notice anything **different** about me?' He gestured to his new human-sized body.

'Have you had a haircut?' Cha Cha replied.

Muzzkito frowned.

'Leave this town alone,' Kung Fu Duck said.

'Nah, I won't be doing that,' Muzzkito said.

'Then we'll have to do this the **HARD** way,' Pow Pow said.

In a **flash,** he spun his rake like a staff and **swung it through the air!**

THWACK!

He sent a group of giant mosquitoes **crashing** to the ground.

'I want a piece of that action,' Kung Fu Duck said. She jumped up and **flicked** her tea towel, knocking another bunch of **MEGA-mozzies** out of the sky.

'That looks like **too much fun**,' Barry said, flinging his rake at a trio of mosquitoes. They crashed to the ground, too!

'I'm joining in, too!' Cha Cha said. She pulled out her Mixy-Fixy, clicked a button and four giant flyswatters sprang out of it!

Cha Cha swung her multi-flyswatter at the mosquitoes. She wiped out a dozen giant mozzies at once!

'What is wrong with you?!'
Muzzkito shouted at the mosquitoes.
'Bomb them!'

The mosquitoes quickly formed into the shape of a **BOMB** and plunged towards us.

'Uh-oh!' said Kenny. 'It looks like this fight is about to **BLOW UP!'**

'The best form of attack is defence,' Pow Pow said.

'And the best type of defence is team defence,' Kung Fu added.

'Let's work together to kick these giant biting bugs to the kerb!' Cha Cha said.

As the massive mosquito bomb drew closer, Pow Pow yelled, **'THREE, TWO, ONE!'**

In unison, the eight of us leapt into the air.

Pow Pow swung his broom.

Barry flung his rake.

Cha Cha wielded her Mixy-Fixy.

And Kung Fu whipped her tea towel.

Us kids got in on the action, too. I did the **biggest** spin kick of my life – five rotations! It brought half a dozen giant mosquitoes **crashing to the ground.**

Kenny exhaled a **huge cloud** of lemon-and-cinnamon breath. It made the mosquitoes so dazed that when Kenny hit them with his pen-swatter, they dropped like flies!

From the moment Sarah got the part of Kung Fu Duck, she carried a tea towel with her everywhere. She could never have imagined she'd get to use it just like the real Kung Fu Duck!

Tiffany's Mixy-Fixy was only a prop, but she spun it so quickly it acted like a propeller, scattering mosquitoes in all directions!

Our team defence was a **HUGE** success. The people of Duck Creek cheered as we knocked every mosquito out of the sky.

Well, all except for **Muzzkito**.

'I'll be back,' **Muzzkito** called down to us. '**Bigger and better than ever!**'

'I wouldn't count on it,' Grandma said, as she returned with her **size converter**.

Before Muzzkito could escape, Grandma turned the **size converter** to **shrink** mode and fired it at him.

ZAP!!!

At first, we thought Muzzkito had disappeared. Then we heard his tiny voice squeaking at Grandma.

You'll pay for this!

WHOOP! WHOOP! WHOOP!

Dr Kane returned in his helicopter.

'Where's Muzzkito?' he bellowed.

'Down here,' Muzzkito shouted in his tiny voice. 'Hurry, Kane, make me **BIG** again!'

'I kept my part of the deal,' Dr Kane bellowed down to him. 'But you've lost your mosquito army, and the people of Duck Creek are still here. **You've failed me!**'

Dr Kane shook his head then flew off into the distance in his helicopter.

'It's time to go back to your own world,' I said to Muzzkito.

'Yeah, we've even **BOOKED** you a spot!' added Kenny.

Before he could argue, I flicked the Character Camera into reverse and pointed it at him.

Just like that, Muzzkito was back in the book. And he didn't seem happy about it!

'We make an **AWESOME** team,' Pow Pow said to us.

'You boys really do look familiar,' Barry the Goat said to me and Kenny. 'You sure we haven't met before?'

'We'd remember if we had!' Kenny said, shooting a nervous look in my direction.

'Really sorry,' I said. 'But H-Dude and I have to run. Hope we get to **save the world** together again one day!'

H-Dude and I quickly got changed and returned to the park as Nelson and Kenny. But the others had gone.

'That's weird,' I said.

'Tiffany and Sarah are probably getting ready for the play,' Kenny said.

'The play!' I said. 'I almost forgot. We're on in half an hour!'

EiGHT

Kenny and I arrived backstage minutes before the play was about to begin. We quickly changed into our costumes and peeked through the curtain. It was a **FULL HOUSE!**

Mum and Grandma were in the front row, smiling and waving. Behind them were four kids in hoodies so baggy we couldn't see their faces.

'Cool hoodies!' Kenny said.

The play started with Kenny as Barry, Sarah as Kung Fu, Tiffany as Cha Cha and me as Pow Pow stepping out of the **time machine.** The audience clapped and cheered.

Kenny was so busy waving to the crowd, he tripped over the bottom of the time machine and went **FLYING** across the stage.

Everyone was worried he'd hurt himself until Kenny **jumped** to his feet.

'A funny goat needs a funny entrance!'

The audience **cracked up** laughing.

One of the kids in the hoodies laughed particularly hard.

After our crazy day fighting Muzzkito, doing the play was a **blast.** Kenny and I **loved** playing Barry and Pow Pow.

And Tiffany and Sarah were so good as Cha Cha and Kung Fu Duck that I almost forgot they weren't the **real thing!**

Even Charles enjoyed his role as Tree Number Three.

When the curtains closed, the audience gave us a **STANDING OVATION.** The kids in the hoodies were particularly enthusiastic!

We were taking off our make-up backstage when the four kids in hoodies approached.

'Congratulations on a **brilliant** show,' one of them said.

'**Best play** I've ever seen!' another added.

Their voices sounded familiar. **Very** familiar. And when they ripped off their hoodies, we realised why!

'What are you all doing here?' I asked, amazed.

'Tiffany and Sarah told us about the play,' Pow Pow said.

'And we couldn't resist seeing how you played us!' Cha Cha said.

'Nailed it!' Barry exclaimed.

'As much as we'd love to stick around,' Pow Pow said, 'it's time for us to go back into the book.'

'Who knows what Muzzkito is getting up to while we're away,' Kung Fu said.

'Do you have the Character Camera?' Pow Pow asked.

'Never leave home without it!' I said, plucking it from my backpack.

We hugged our heroes and said our goodbyes.

'If you see Ninja Kid and H-Dude,' Pow Pow said, 'tell them we're sorry we didn't get to say a proper goodbye.'

'Will do,' I replied. Then I opened the book and zapped Pow Pow, Kung Fu, Barry and Cha Cha.

We stared in amazement at the book, which once again featured our awesome new friends.

THE END!

READ THEM ALL!

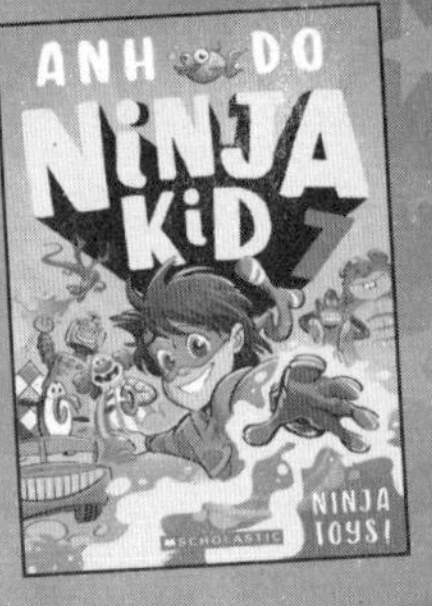

NINJA KID 11 COMING SOON!